CONTENTS

All words in **bold** can be found in the glossary on page 31.

WHO WERE KNIGHTS?

The year is 1250, in **medieval times**. Europe is a chaotic, dangerous place full of robbers, raiders and bands of fighting armies. Knights are the toughest warriors around: strong, skilful and brave in battle. They are the trusted champions of powerful kings and lords who employ knights to serve them. The knights defend and protect their lords' castles and conquer new lands.

KNIGHTS IN SHINING ARMOUR

Knights were no ordinary soldiers. These elite fighters used huge swords, wore suits of gleaming armour from head-to-toe and fought on the backs of large and powerful warhorses.

AMAZING FACT
The first knights

In 800 CE, Charlemagne became the emperor of central and western Europe. In an attempt to stop invaders, he used mounted warriors and rewarded them with land if they fought for him. These were the first knights. Knights and castles became common in Britain when William the Conqueror of Normandy, France, defeated King Harold at the Battle of Hastings in 1066 and became King of England.

KNIGHTS

James Nixon

W

ANKLIN WATTS

Franklin Watts
338 Euston Road
London NW1 3BH

Franklin Watts Australia
Level 17/207 Kent Street
Sydney, NSW 2000

This edition © Franklin Watts 2014

Series editor: Amy Stephenson
Planning and production by Discovery Books Ltd
Editor: James Nixon
Series designer: D.R. ink
Picture researcher: James Nixon

Picture credits: cover image (Nejron Photo/
Shutterstock)Alamy: pp. 7 top (Louise Heusinkveld), 8 top
(Classic Image), 9 (P Seplavy), 16 (Tim Gainey), 18 bottom (The Art Archive), 19 bottom
(Detail Heritage), 25 (The Art Archive), 27 (legge). Corbis: pp. 26 (Lebrecht Music & Arts),
29 top (Richard T Nowitz). Getty: pp. 8 bottom (French School), 21 (SuperStock),
22 (Stock Montage), 23 bottom (DEGAS Jean-Pierre). Shutterstock: pp. 2 & 18 top
(Rob Hainer), 4 (PLRANG), 6 (Istvan Csak), 7 bottom (Lowe R Llaguno), 10 (Nejron
Photo), 11 top (AMC Photography), 12 Robert H Creigh), 13 top-left (Yingko), 13 top-2nd
from left (EchoArt), 13 top-right (Creative HQ), 13 bottom (Litvin Leonid), 14 (Raulin),
15 top (Stefano Panzeri), 15 bottom (Marco Richter), 17 top (PLRANG), 17 bottom
(antipathique), 20 top, 20 middle (khd), 20 bottom (St Nick), 23 top (Ed Phillips), 24
main (Abramova Kseniya), 24 bottom-left (Lyubov Timofeyeva), 28 (Raulin), 29 bottom
(Jose Gil), 30 (Boykov). Wikimedia: pp. 5 both, 11 bottom, 13 top-2nd from right, 19 top.

Dewey number: 355'.00902
ISBN: 978 1 4451 3562 5

A CIP catalogue record for this book is available from the British Library
Printed in China

Franklin Watts is a division of Hachette Children's Books,
an Hachette UK company.
www.hachette.co.uk

THE STARS OF THE SHOW

Being a knight was not a job for a coward. Every time knights rode into battle they risked being killed. However, being a knight also brought great riches. Kings rewarded them for their work with treasures, land and castles. Knights could expect fame, honour and glory. To show respect for their high rank, knights were called 'Sir'. Many young men dreamed of becoming a knight and women admired their heroes – they were quite simply the stars of the show.

TRUE OR FALSE?

Knights lost their importance once gunpowder had been invented. **True or False?**

TRUE! The skills of a knight were pretty useless when one shot to the head was enough to kill him!

AMAZING FACT
Famous knights

Perhaps the most famous knights were those that served King Arthur, even though no one knows if they really existed. The legend says that the knights, including Sir Lancelot and Sir Galahad, gathered at a round table (right) in a place called Camelot. Sir Galahad succeeded in his heroic quest to find the precious stone cup called the **Holy Grail** (below).

William Marshal, born in 1147, was definitely a real knight. He rose through the ranks to serve four kings of England – Henry II, Richard the Lionheart, John and Henry III. He has been described as the greatest knight that ever lived. He was a master at winning tournaments, which at that time were deadly and bloody battles.

BECOMING A KNIGHT

Only a select group of men became knights. The lucky ones were usually the sons of wealthy **nobles**, or had fathers who were knights themselves. Men from ordinary families were sometimes made knights if they had shown great bravery in battle.

THE LIFE OF A PAGE

Training to be a knight was a long, hard process. It usually began at the age of seven, at which time the boy was sent to live in a lord's castle. Young trainees were known as pages. A wealthy lord would have many pages. As well as learning how to ride, handle horses and use weapons, pages were taught good manners and how to read and write.

The most important thing for a page was to develop his fitness and strength. Pages trained with heavy wooden swords and shields, to build up their muscles. They learned how to hunt using hawks and with a bow and arrow. As they trained they worked as household servants, serving meals and doing jobs no one else wanted. Trainees that cleaned the stables were called grooms.

TRUE OR FALSE?

Pages fought on piggyback to practise mounted combat. **True or False?**

TRUE! They developed their skills while balanced on each other's shoulders

Young men who wanted to be knights practised constantly to improve their skills with weapons such as the bow.

THE LIFE OF A SQUIRE

At the age of 14 a page became a squire and acted as a personal assistant to a knight. Squires were allowed to handle more dangerous weapons as they grew from boys into men. The squire looked after the knight's equipment and helped him dress up in his armour before battle. He then accompanied his master on the battlefield.

Squires had to replace a knight's weapons if they were broken or dropped and replace his horse if it was injured. If the knight was taken prisoner the squire had to attempt a rescue. It was a dangerous life and many squires came under fire from arrows and were killed.

There was a pecking order among squires. The 'squire of the body' was the closest to the knight and the most trusted to accompany the knight in battle.

AMAZING FACT
The spinning quintain

A squire had to become skilled at using the lance on horseback. The lance was a long wooden pole with a metal spike on the end. Target practice involved charging at a quintain. After hitting the shield on one end of the quintain the squire had to duck immediately as a heavy weight or sack on the other end of the pole would swing round and could knock him off his horse!

WINNING YOUR SPURS

After many long years of training, the squire became a lean and mean fighting machine. Not all squires could manage it, but if they proved themselves, at the age of 21 they were ready to become a knight. All that was left for a squire to do was to take part in a special ceremony where he would be awarded his own sword and **spurs**. Squires that had shown great courage in battle were sometimes knighted at a much younger age.

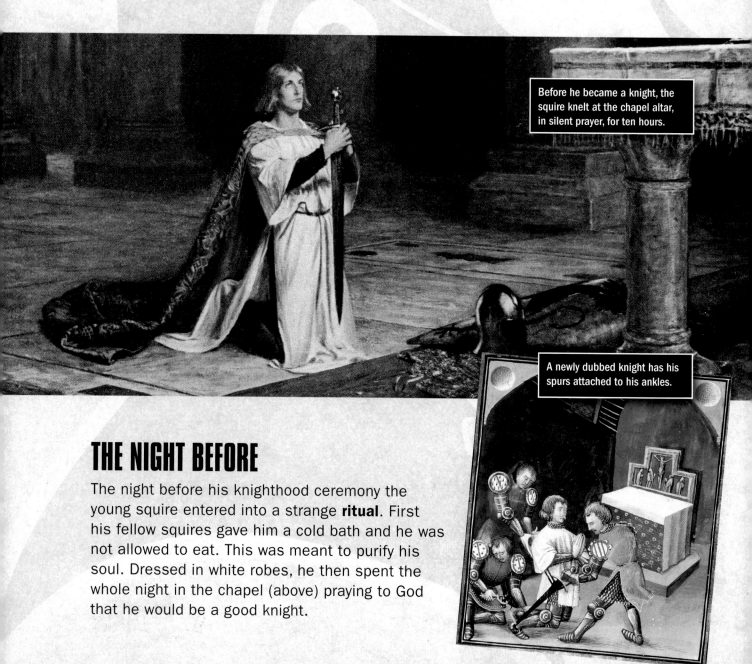

Before he became a knight, the squire knelt at the chapel altar, in silent prayer, for ten hours.

A newly dubbed knight has his spurs attached to his ankles.

THE NIGHT BEFORE

The night before his knighthood ceremony the young squire entered into a strange **ritual**. First his fellow squires gave him a cold bath and he was not allowed to eat. This was meant to purify his soul. Dressed in white robes, he then spent the whole night in the chapel (above) praying to God that he would be a good knight.

THE DUBBING CEREMONY

In the morning the young squire dressed in his smartest tunic and cloak, and headed to the great hall of the castle or to an outdoor ceremony to be dubbed. The dubbing was when the squire officially became a knight. A local knight, noble, or even the king took the squire's sword, tapped him on each shoulder with it, and said 'Arise, Sir Knight'. The newly dubbed knight then had a sword strapped to his waist and spurs fastened to his ankles.

AMAZING FACT
Losing your spurs

In the dubbing ceremony the knight vowed to be a faithful and devoted knight. He swore to defend the church, orphans, the weak and widows. Should a knight fail in his duties, behave badly, or be cowardly on the battlefield he was punished. In a different ceremony a disgraced knight would have his spurs hacked off by the king's cook with a chopping knife. His shield was then hung upside down as a sign of shame.

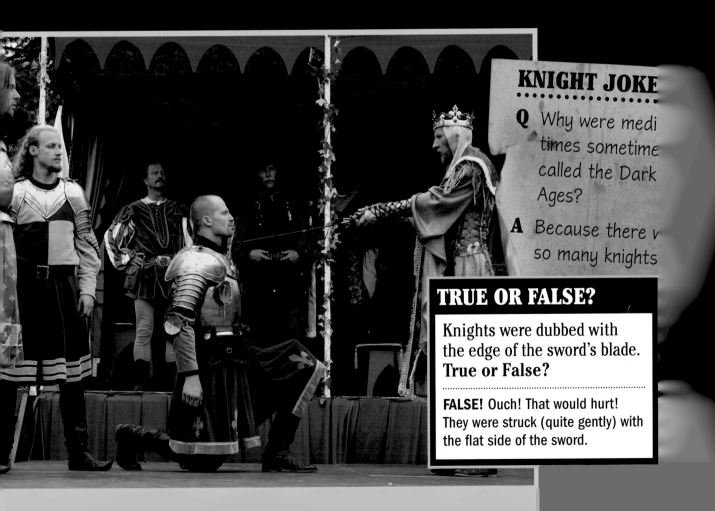

KNIGHT JOKE

Q Why were medi[...] times sometime[...] called the Dark Ages?

A Because there v[...] so many knights[...]

TRUE OR FALSE?

Knights were dubbed with the edge of the sword's blade. **True or False?**

FALSE! Ouch! That would hurt! They were struck (quite gently) with the flat side of the sword.

DRESSED TO KILL

Some knights were rich enough to afford the expensive, tailor-made suits of armour that protected them during battle. During the 1100s knights wore a suit of chain mail made from thousands of tiny iron rings linked together. By the 1400s they wore solid, metal-plated armour with padded garments and chain mail beneath.

A LIVING FORTRESS

Well-made armour was almost indestructible – any dents could be hammered back into shape. Each plate of metal overlapped the next for maximum protection but it was surprisingly easy to move in. It did have its down sides though. Getting dressed was complicated. The squire always put the plates on the knight from the feet upwards, finishing with the helmet. Running around in heavy, clanking armour was also hot and very tiring. And even when wearing the best armour, you still had to fight for your life.

AMAZING FACT
Making chain mail

Chain mail (below) looked like a piece of knitting except it was made of metal. Making it was an extremely time consuming job for the local **blacksmith**. Each and every ring was stamped out of a sheet of iron. These were then linked to each other with **rivets** to hold them in place.

TRUE OR FALSE?

Knights had to be lifted on to their horses because their armour was so heavy. **True or False?**

FALSE! However, a suit of armour did weigh between 15 and 25 kilograms.

THE RIGHT EQUIPMENT

Plate-armour covered the knight from top to bottom. A leather-covered, wooden shield added to this defence.

Helmet – a detachable visor covers the face. There are narrow slits for the eyes.

Shoulder guards

Breastplate – with a matching backplate at the rear

Couters – elbow guards

Gauntlets – gloves with ringed, metal plates over the fingers

Cuisses – buckled on to the thighs

Chain mail – protects small places not covered by armour, such as the back of the neck and under the arms

Poleyns – protected the knee caps

Greaves – protected the lower leg

Sabatons – foot guards

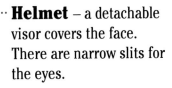

AMAZING FACT
Changing fashions

Plate armour was often made to look fashionable as well as protect. Some armours were painted or had gold plating added to the borders for decoration. In the early 1500s German armour had ridges in it to copy the pleated clothing that was popular at the time. This style (left) was called 'Maximilian' after the German emperor.

ARMED AND DANGEROUS

A knight owned many weapons but the most important in battle were his lance and sword. On horseback the pointed lance, measuring over three metres long, was the weapon of choice for charging and piercing the enemy. On the ground the knight needed expert and swift sword skills. A knight kept a single-handed sword on his body at all times. The sword was good for slashing as it had double-edged blades. Later on, swords were made stronger and thicker with a diamond-shaped point that could thrust through the rings of a victim's chain mail.

The lance was a lethal weapon, especially when knights were charging on their horses at up to 100 kph (60 mph).

KNIGHT JOKE

Q Did you hear about the knight who had his left side cut off?

A He's all right now!

TRUE OR FALSE?

Knights sprayed their swords with snake venom so that a wound would lead to certain death. **True or False?**

TRUE! But they had to be careful not to poison themselves.

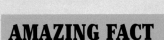

AMAGING FACT

Armour-crunching weapons

Some weapons were heavy and awkward to carry. But they more than made up for it with their awesome power. A two-handed longsword was more than a metre long and weighed up to two kilograms. It could cut through a man's helmet – and skull! The lethal mace dealt deadly blows from close range. It had a heavy metal head on the end of a shaft and could smash a knight's brains out.

Two-handed longsword

Mace

Poleaxe

Flail

CLOSE COMBAT

Other weapons were good if a knight was brave enough to get close to his enemy. A small, thin sword or an even smaller sharp dagger were handy for stabbing an enemy through a chink in their armour. A battle-axe had a wedge-shaped blade and short wooden handle. One swing of this could slice through an enemy's limbs. The poleaxe had many uses. This curved axe was good for slashing and grappling and the spike on the top was effective against a mounted enemy. A flail had a spiky iron ball on the end of each chain and could shatter bones.

MISSILES

A battle-axe could also be hurled as a missile. There were also specially designed throwing axes which could smash through armour and shields. The knight would swing the axe around and over his head to gather speed before letting it go, like a hammer thrower in the Olympic Games.

Two knights fight each other with battle-axes.

WARHORSES

Horses were an important part of a knight's life and vital on the battlefield. Warhorses were powerful, aggressive creatures. They were massive animals measuring up to two-and-a-half metres high. The horses had to get used to the smell of blood and the noise of battle. They also had to be strong enough to carry knights plus their weapons and armour.

TRUE OR FALSE?

Knights put scary masks on the faces of their warhorses to frighten the enemy. **True or False?**

FALSE! But a spiky horn was sometimes added to the head armour which made the horse look like a unicorn.

KNIGHT JOKE

Q What did a knight give to his sick warhorse?

A Cough stirrup!

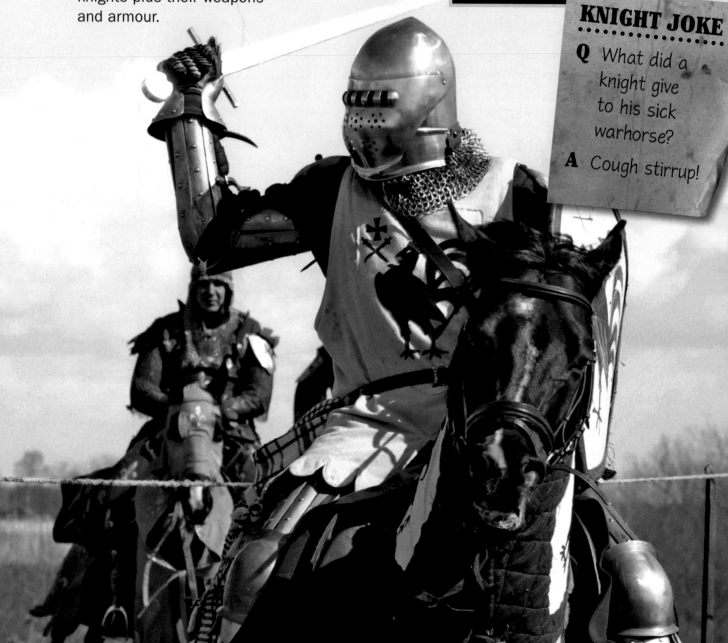

THE RIGHT HORSE FOR THE RIGHT JOB

A rich knight owned three types of horses. His heavy warhorse was called a destrier. For travelling, a knight would have a more comfortable, gentle horse called a palfrey. A courser was an expensive horse. It was super quick, perfect for hunting and carrying messages.

READY FOR BATTLE

A warhorse was sometimes protected by rigid pieces of plate-armour called barding on its head, neck and chest. The rear of the horse was covered with padded cloth. The high pommel and cantle (below) of the saddle made it difficult for enemies to knock a knight off his horse.

Riders in battle had to be aware of enemy traps. Upturned stakes and iron spikes called caltrops could pierce a horse's hooves. Enemies also dug pits and covered them over with grass.

AMAZING FACT
Trained to kill

Warhorses were highly trained. A knight needed his hands to wield his weapons so he would squeeze his legs and use his spurs (below) to control the horse. The horse could be commanded to charge, trample on fallen bodies, and even kick and bite the enemy.

Cantle

Pommel

GOING INTO BATTLE

In times of war a king would call on his knights and the armies under their command to fight. Much was at stake on the battlefield. A defeat could mean the loss of a territory. Knights faced many different types of fighters as well as other knights. Most enemies were foot soldiers. They were less well equipped than knights, but they fought hard for their lives. Battles were fierce. Even if a knight survived he would lose many fellow knights.

AMAZING FACT
Battle of Agincourt

At the battle of Agincourt in 1415, English knights scored a famous victory over the French despite being outnumbered by four to one. It was mainly thanks to the English **longbowmen**. As the French knights tried to cross a muddy field they were bombarded with a terrifying hail of arrows. Thousands of French knights were killed or taken prisoner.

KNIGHT JOKE

Q When a knight in armour was killed what did they put on his grave?

A Rust in Peace!

FOOT SOLDIERS

Foot soldiers armed themselves with wooden clubs, pitchforks and **pikes**. They used **halberds** for attacking knights on their horses. A halberd was a strong spear with an axe-like blade fixed to it.

Archers were another type of foot soldier. These were tricky for knights as they could fire a deadly rain of arrows from far away. A skilled longbowman could fire ten to twelve arrows per minute and hit a target from over 200 metres away. Crossbows were even more dangerous. They shot metal bolts that could smash through armour.

THE CAVALRY CHARGE

But knights were the most feared force on the battlefield. They charged their horses in close formation with their lances held out in front of them. Dozens of foot soldiers could be cut down in seconds. Soldiers struck down, even if only slightly hurt, were likely to be trampled by horses following behind.

AMAZING FACT
Coats of arms

In the heat of battle how did knights dressed in armour know who their enemies were? Each knight had his own coat of arms. This would be worn as a badge on his shield and was also often sewn into his surcoat (a cloth garment worn on top of the armour). Only certain colours and styles were allowed to be used. The coat of arms passed to his eldest son when a knight died. Other children used variants of their father's arms.

TRUE OR FALSE?

Some foot soldiers used to run into the middle of the battle to collect up all the spare arrows. **True or False?**

TRUE! They were called retrievers.

LOYALTY TO THE KING

Kings and lords valued a knight's loyalty as much as his fighting skills. Knights promised to be faithful and serve their lord or the king at all times even if it meant risking their own lives. In return for a knight's service the king gave him land. This was part of an arrangement known as the feudal system.

THE FEUDAL SYSTEM

Everyone knew their place in medieval times:
- The king owned all of the land.
- The king granted important lords and **barons** their own lands. These nobles in return provided trained soldiers to fight for the king.
- Lords and barons gave away some of their land to professional fighters called knights.
- The land was worked on by **peasants**.

A knight was prepared to fight to the death to defend his lord or the king.

A knight kneels before his king.

KNIGHT JOKE

Q What was Camelot famous for?

A Its knight life!

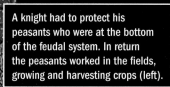

A knight had to protect his peasants who were at the bottom of the feudal system. In return the peasants worked in the fields, growing and harvesting crops (left).

LOOKING AFTER THE PEASANTS

Knights had many duties in peacetime as well as war. The land a knight was given had to be managed. A knight spent a lot of time giving out orders to the peasants. He was also supposed to protect them and keep law and order. A knight served as judge to settle arguments between neighbours. He also made sure that the **taxes** were collected, which didn't make him popular. Knights that served the king directly had to be a good friend and offer the king advice when it was asked for.

TRUE OR FALSE?

Women could not become knights because they were not strong enough. **True or False?**

FALSE! Between 1358 and 1488, it is recorded that 68 women were dubbed as knights in Britain.

AMAZING FACT
Taking the Oath

The knight's promise to serve the lord was a key part of the feudal system. A knight swore the Oath of Fealty, saying the words: 'I promise on my faith that I will in the future be faithful to the lord, never cause him harm and will respect him completely against all persons in good faith and without **deceit**'. The knight also called for punishment from God if he broke the oath. If a knight did break his promise the king could order him to be thrown into jail or even have his head chopped off!

Knight's often placed their hand on holy relics when they swore an oath.

LIFE IN A CASTLE

To be given his own castle was a knight's greatest reward. If a knight was not given a castle by the king or queen he could always capture one or build his own if he had pots of money. Once a knight had a castle he had to keep it well repaired and guard it night and day. These magnificent fortresses were attractive to enemy armies.

CUNNING CASTLES

The central keep of the castle was protected by an outer wall with towers spaced along it. The walls were several metres thick and archers could fire from the **battlements** to stop invaders in their tracks. If an enemy made it across the **moat** and **drawbridge**, a heavy oak door and **portcullis** still stood in their way. The portcullis was a heavy iron grill with spikes on the bottom that came crashing down in the gateway.

Battlements

Keep

Tower

Outer wall

Portcullis

AMAZING FACT

Largest castle

The biggest castle in the UK is Windsor (left). It was built by William the Conqueror in the 11th century and has been used by British monarchs since Henry I lived there in 1110. Today, the Queen still uses it as her weekend home. The castle covers a gigantic area measuring about 55,000 square metres.

A PLACE TO LIVE AND WORK

Hundreds of people lived and worked inside a castle. A person called the steward was in charge of all the servants who cleaned, cooked and ran errands. There were many workshops where goods such as a knight's weapons and armour were made or repaired. Chickens and pigs were kept inside the walls to provide fresh food. The knight's family had private rooms and were the only people who slept in beds. For most, castle life was uncomfortable. In winter it was cold, draughty and damp.

TRUE OR FALSE?

There were no toilets in a castle so people used the well. **True or False?**

FALSE! The well was used for fresh water! People sat on a wooden seat called a garderobe and the waste fell down a chute into the moat.

AMAZING FACT

Grand feasts

Everyone dined together in the great hall. If there were special guests huge feasts could start in the morning and last all day. The most important people sat at the top table using silver plates. Everyone else ate off big slices of stale bread! **Jesters**, actors and musicians entertained the crowd. There was always a lot of meat on the menu – anything that had been hunted, including gulls, swans, peacocks and seals. Sometimes, a food taster nibbled the food before it was served to check that nothing had been poisoned!

SIEGE

Knights and their armies would lay **siege** to enemy castles in an attempt to capture them. During a siege the army used huge war machines to try to smash their way in. If they failed they surrounded the castle and simply waited until the enemy's food or water ran out. The people inside could choose to surrender or starve to death. Sieges could drag on for weeks or months.

KNIGHT JOKE

Q What was a medieval insomniac called?

A A sleepless knight!

WAR MACHINES

Attackers scaled ladders or built giant siege towers (left) in an attempt to get behind the castle walls. A battering ram made from a tree trunk was swung back and forth to break down the castle door or the corners of the castle. It took up to 100 soldiers to operate a ram and great skill was needed in timing the swing.

Catapults were used to hurl lumps of rock into the castle. The mangonel launched heavy stones from a bowl-shaped bucket up to 400 metres away. The mighty trebuchet flung boulders from a sling at the end of a long wooden arm.

TRUE OR FALSE?

War machines such as the mangonel were built on the spot during the siege. **True or False?**

TRUE! They were far too big to move long distances.

WATCH OUT!

Sieges were dangerous and difficult. Castles were designed to be defended from attack. Machines such as the battering ram had to be covered in animal skin to give the attackers operating the ram protection. Defenders pelted the attackers with stone missiles through the gaps in the battlements, while archers fired arrows through narrow slits in the walls (left).

Murder holes were particularly nasty. Through these holes in the ceiling, defenders poured red-hot sand or boiling water on to the attacking soldiers' heads. Many traps were set outside the castle. Dried grass was set on fire with flaming arrows just as the invaders approached. Ditches were dug into the ground to topple the siege towers.

AMAGING FACT
Dirty tactics

If the defenders were holding out longer than expected there were some cunning tricks knights could use to speed up their surrender. Digging tunnels under the castle walls and then starting a fire in them caused the castle to crumble and collapse. Another idea was to spread sickness in the castle. The attackers could pollute the castle's water supply with rotting **corpses** or even catapult dead bodies of humans, rats and cows into the castle to spread disease!

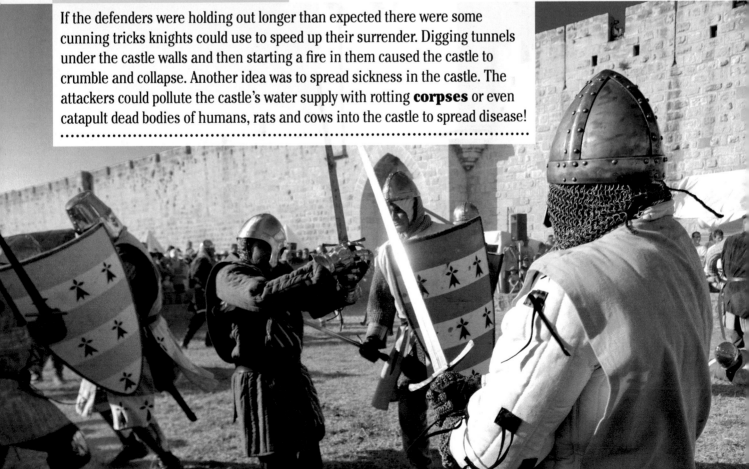

CRUSADES ABROAD

Crusades abroad kept knights busy. A crusade was a huge march into foreign countries to control holy lands and gain more power and wealth. The crusaders would also spread their Christian beliefs. The battles often lasted less than a day but it could take months for the knights to reach their destination.

TRUE OR FALSE?

A crusader knight shared his tent with his horse. **True or False?**

TRUE! It must have been cosy!

THE ROAD TO BATTLE

The crusaders travelled slowly as most were on foot. Crusades usually started in spring because in winter it was too snowy and wet. On the road to battle, armies had to carry all their weapons, armour and other supplies. Crusaders sometimes had to travel to war by ship. Journeys were perilous. Knights might have to cross snowy mountains or scorching deserts. At sea there was the risk of shipwreck. Life in an army camp was only for the toughest. The tents were smelly and damp. The food was foul and the water was dirty. Soldiers also had to cope with fleas, rats and other pests. Many died from fever and sickness.

A crusader-built fortress, near Taba, in Egypt.

A determined and excited crusader sets off to conquer new lands.

In 1098, on route to Jerusalem, crusaders captured the walled city of Antioch, in modern-day Turkey.

A HOLY CRUSADE

European warriors and knights got together to launch their first crusade to the Middle East in 1096. The goal was to take over the holy city of Jerusalem, but the travelling army did not reach there until 7 May 1099! Many cities and forts had to be invaded along the way. The battles were bloody, causing death and destruction on a huge scale. Many more knights died due to the lack of water around Jerusalem. Out of the 7,500 knights who marched to Jerusalem only about 1,500 survived. After capturing Jerusalem the city was retaken by the Muslims in 1187 and many other crusades failed to take it back.

AMAZING FACT
Looting

It sounds cruel but travelling armies raided towns and villages on their route. Ordinary people hid in horror as soldiers smashed into their homes. The army of men stole whatever they could grab. Food was vital as it was usually in short supply. Towns had riches to steal, from jewels and fine crafts found in shops to the silver and gold treasures in churches.

THE CODE OF CHIVALRY

A mark of a good knight was not just how well they fought but how well they behaved. Knights were supposed to follow a strict code of conduct called chivalry although in reality most knights didn't live up to this ideal. The word chivalry comes from the French word *chevalier* meaning knight. Chivalry began in the 1100s and instructed knights to be polite, honest, generous, and to treat everyone with respect – especially women.

COURTLY LOVE

Knights were meant to be well-mannered and charming in the company of women. They dedicated their **honourable** deeds to a particular lady. Surprisingly the rules allowed knights and ladies to admire each other even if they were already married to someone else. A knight would do heroic things to demonstrate his love. In return the lady would give the knight a token of her love, such as a glove or scarf, for him to wear during a tournament. This was called 'courtly love'.

BE BRAVE

The protection of the poor, the weak and children, and the defence of the church was another part of the code that knights obeyed. To show this, knights had to be incredibly brave. In fact some people would say that knights were slightly crazy. A knight was never meant to turn his back on the enemy and run away, or abandon a friend who was in serious trouble.

King Arthur's chief knight, Sir Lancelot, declares his love for Arthur's wife, Queen Guinevere.

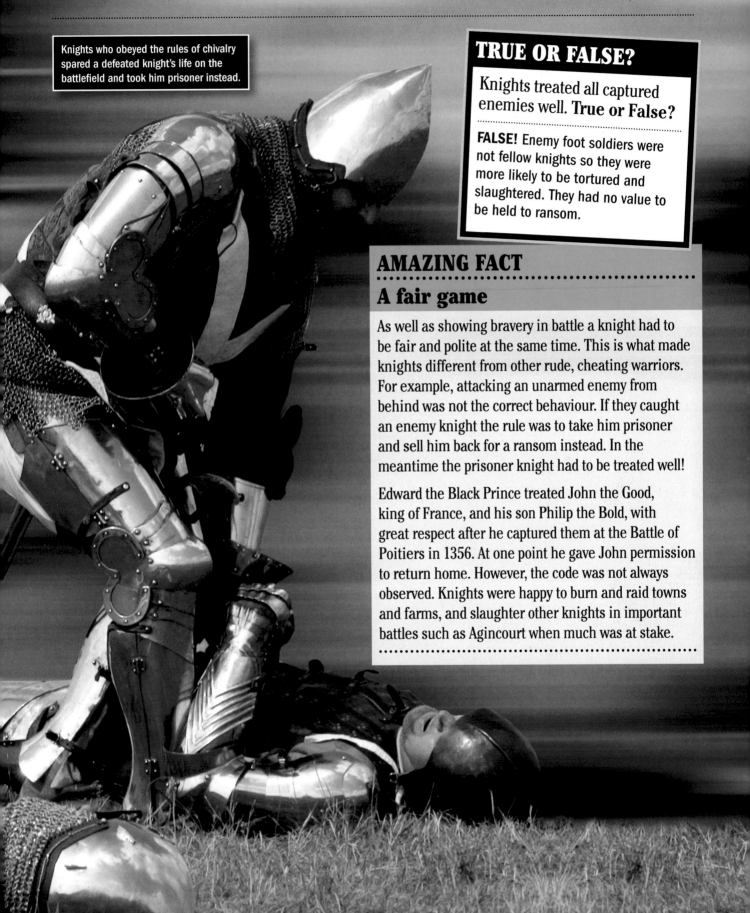

Knights who obeyed the rules of chivalry spared a defeated knight's life on the battlefield and took him prisoner instead.

TRUE OR FALSE?

Knights treated all captured enemies well. **True or False?**

FALSE! Enemy foot soldiers were not fellow knights so they were more likely to be tortured and slaughtered. They had no value to be held to ransom.

AMAZING FACT

A fair game

As well as showing bravery in battle a knight had to be fair and polite at the same time. This is what made knights different from other rude, cheating warriors. For example, attacking an unarmed enemy from behind was not the correct behaviour. If they caught an enemy knight the rule was to take him prisoner and sell him back for a ransom instead. In the meantime the prisoner knight had to be treated well!

Edward the Black Prince treated John the Good, king of France, and his son Philip the Bold, with great respect after he captured them at the Battle of Poitiers in 1356. At one point he gave John permission to return home. However, the code was not always observed. Knights were happy to burn and raid towns and farms, and slaughter other knights in important battles such as Agincourt when much was at stake.

JOUSTS AND TOURNAMENTS

Tournaments were a knight's chance to win fame, glory and big prizes. It also kept his skills sharp so he was ready for war. There were different types of tournament from mock battles (above) to duels and jousts. Lots of spectators turned up to watch, including powerful nobles and attractive ladies, so it was important for the knight to put on a good show.

MAD MOCK BATTLES

Tournaments were rowdy, exciting events. In a mock battle, knights were divided into two sides. The fighting was supposed to be friendly but it usually ended up being fierce and bloody. A defeated knight could lose his horse and armour. A tournament could last for days and at night there was feasting – for those that were still alive!

KNIGHT JOKE

Q What do you call a knight who likes to joust?

A Lance a lot!

TRUE OR FALSE?

Lances were measured in a tournament to make sure that all knights had the same length lance. **True or False?**

TRUE! After all, chivalry demands fair play and no cheating.

BONE-JANGLING JOUSTS

Jousting tournaments saw knights challenge each other one-on-one. Armed knights charged at one another at full speed on their horses. Each tried to knock the other flying with his lance. Points could also be scored for a good hit or for breaking a lance against the other knight. The prize money for the resulting winner could be huge.

Tournaments were great entertainments that had to be well planned and prepared for. Grandstands and tents were erected around the arena, which was usually close to the castle so people could watch from the battlements. The rules and style of tournament were announced from the castle and town criers then spread the word. Messages were sent out to knights challenging them to enter. Jousting events were often part of great occasions. For example, a tournament was arranged to celebrate Henry VIII's marriage to his new Queen, Catherine of Aragon, in 1509.

AMAZING FACT
Blunted weapons

The number of cracked skulls and dead bodies that piled up at tournaments angered kings who were losing their knights. In 1292 new laws were made for tournaments that meant swords and lances had to be blunted. Even so, broken bones and deaths were still common. Medics were always on hand, but they had some odd cures. A red-hot iron was used to stop a wound bleeding and the bandages they used were soaked in egg to seal the wound!

QUIZ

How much have you learned from reading this book? Here is a quiz to test your memory.

1. How did kings reward knights that fought for them?

2. At what age did a page usually become a squire?

3. What is a dubbing ceremony?

4. What is chain mail made from?

5. What is the name for the foot guards in a suit of armour?

6. How long is a lance?

7. Which weapon has a spiky iron ball on the end of each chain?

8. What was a knight's quickest horse called?

9. Which type of foot soldier killed many French knights at the Battle of Agincourt (1415)?

10. Who was at the bottom of the feudal system?

11. What is a portcullis?

12. How far can a mangonel launch lumps of rock?

13. Why did crusaders loot ordinary people's homes?

14. How were knights supposed to treat their prisoners?

15. In a jousting competition how could a knight score points?

GLOSSARY

baron a nobleman who is given land by the king

battlements a low wall at the top of a castle with openings for defenders to shoot through

blacksmith a person who makes and repairs iron objects

corpse a dead body

deceit if you are dishonest or trick someone you are deceiving, or showing deceit

drawbridge a bridge over a moat that has a hinge at one end so it can be raised and lowered

halberd a weapon with an axe-like blade and a steel spike mounted on the end of a long shaft

Holy Grail a legendary, sacred cup or dish, which Jesus Christ is said to have drank from

honourable an honourable person is honest and behaves in the proper manner

longbowmen archers that used large bows to fire long arrows from over 200 metres away

jester a professional joker

medieval times relating to the Middle Ages, a period of history between the 5th and 15th centuries

moat a defensive ditch filled with water surrounding a castle

noble a member of the highest class in society

peasant a member of the lowest class in medieval society who farmed the land

pike a weapon with a spearhead on a long wooden shaft

portcullis a heavy, metal grill that slides down grooves on each side of a gateway to block it

ritual a ceremony involving a set series of actions

rivet a short, metal pin for holding two metal pieces together

siege use an army to surround an enemy building

spurs a device with a spike worn on a rider's heel to urge a horse forward

taxes the money that a government charges its people

WANT TO KNOW MORE?

Here are some places where you can find out a lot more about knights:

WEBSITES

www.medieval-life-and-times.info
Find out about medieval weapons, castles and knights and much more.

www.medieval-castle-siege-weapons.com
This site is full of articles describing how castles were sieged.

www.youtube.com/watch?v=hVY3gdqxvB0
Watch some jousting action.

BOOKS

Knight, Christopher Gravett, (Dorling Kindersley, 2012)

Greatest Warriors: Knights, Peter Heppelwhite, (Franklin Watts, 2014)

Medieval Knights, Charlotte Guillain, (Raintree, 2011)

Knights and Castles (series), Paul Humphrey and Laura Durman, (Franklin Watts, 2013)

The Tale of the Cid: and Other Stories of Knights and Chivalry, Andrew Lang, (Dover Publications, 2012)

History Crafts: Knights, Neil Morris, (Franklin Watts, 2013)

Tracking Down: Medieval Life in Britain, Moira Butterfield, (Franklin Watts, 2010)

Website disclaimer:
Note to parents and teachers: Every effort has been made by the Publishers to ensure that these websites are suitable for children, that they are of the highest educational value, and that they contain no inappropriate or offensive material. However, because of the nature of the Internet, it is impossible to guarantee that the contents of these sites will not be altered. We strongly advise that Internet access is supervised by a responsible adult.

INDEX